Salty Flavour

BBQ Spice Rub

Rice Seasoning

Taco Seasoning Sea Salt Style 6

Greek Seasoning 7

Hawaiian Seasoning 8

Delicious Steak Rub 9

Quick and Easy Taco Seasoning 10

Homemade Garam Masala Seasoning 11

Criollo Seasoning 12

Delicious Taco Seasoning 13

Cajun Spice 14

Quick Cajun Seasoning 15

Chicken Seasoning Spicy Style 16

Sage Infused Italian Seasoning 17

Meat Seasoning 18

Cumin Taco Seasoning 19

Buttermilk Dressing 20

Chili-Free Taco Seasoning 21

Easy Apple Pie Seasoning 22

Mild Curry Seasoning 23

Mediterranean Spice Mix 24

Spanish Seasoning 25

BBQ Chili Rub 26

Hungarian Paprika-Chili-Mix 27

Tasty Pizza Topping 28

Hellenic Seasoning 29

Chicken Seasoning 30

Rural Style Dressing 31

Paprika-Thyme-Seasoning	32
Bread Crumbs Seasoning	33
Tex-Mex Seasoning	34
Onion-Garlic-Chilistyle-Mix	35
Burger Seasoning	36
Pumpkin Pie Flavour	37
Acadia Spices	38
Chicken Rub	39
Seafood Friendly Seasoning	40
Herb Salt	41
Lamb Rub	42
Chili Seasoning Blend	43
Mare Mediterraneum Seasoning	44
Pickling Spices	45
Ground Beef Taco Seasoning	46
Oatmeal Flavour	47
Fish Seasoning	48
Carribean Curry Blend	49
Ginger-Garlic-Paste	50
Popcorn Seasoning	51
Pinyin Five-Spices	52

Salty Flavour

Ingredients:

2 Tbsp. of Salt

2 tsp. of White Sugar

¾ tsp. of Paprika

¼ tsp. of Ground Turmeric

¼ tsp. of Onion Powder

¼ tsp. of Garlic Powder

¼ tsp. of Cornstarch

Directions:

1. In a small mixing bowl, mix all of the ingredients together well.
2. Use a food processor to blend it very well.
3. Store it in an airtight container.

BBQ Spice Rub

Ingredients:

80 g of Paprika

45 g of Pepper

60 g of Brown Sugar

2 Tbsp. of Chili Powder

2 Tbsp. of Garlic Powder

2 Tbsp. of Onion Powder

1 Tbsp. of Sea Salt

2 tsp. of Cayenne Pepper

Directions:

1. In a small mixing bowl, mix all of the ingredients together well.
2. Store it in an airtight container.

Rice Seasoning

Ingredients:

70 g of Salt

2 Tbsp. of White Sugar

2 tsp. of Paprika – Smoked

1 tsp. of Garlic Powder

1 ½ tsp. of Onion Powder

½ tsp. of White Pepper

½ tsp. of Turmeric

¼ tsp. of Thyme

Directions:

1. In a small mixing bowl, mix all of the ingredients together well.
2. Store it in an airtight container.
3. Use your food processor if you want it blended thoroughly.

Taco Seasoning Sea Salt Style

Ingredients:

1 Clove of Garlic – Peeled, Minced

1 tsp. of Sea Salt

1 Tbsp. of Chili Powder

¼ tsp. of Red Pepper Flakes

¼ tsp. of Oregano

½ tsp. of Paprika

1 ½ tsp. of Cumin

1 tsp. of Pepper

Directions:

1. In a small mixing bowl, mix all of the ingredients together well.
2. Store it in an airtight container.

Greek Seasoning

Ingredients:

1 ½ tsp. of Oregano

1 tsp. of Thyme

½ tsp. of Basil

½ tsp. of Marjoram

½ tsp. of Minced Onion – Dried

¼ tsp. of Minced Garlic – Dried

Directions:

1. In a small mixing bowl, mix all of the ingredients together well.
2. Store it in an airtight container.
3. Good for 6 months.

Hawaiian Seasoning

Ingredients:

3 Tbsp. of Coarsely Ground Pepper

3 Tbsp. of Ground Cumin

1 ½ tsp. of Turmeric

1 tsp. of Cardamom

1 tsp. of Sumac

¼ tsp. of Salt

Directions:

1. In a small mixing bowl, mix all of the ingredients together well.
2. Use a food processor to blend it very well.
3. Store it in an airtight container.

Delicious Steak Rub

Ingredients:

2 ½ tsp. of Ground Cinnamon

2 tsp. of Oregano

1 tsp. of Chili Powder

1 tsp. of Cumin

1 tsp. of Salt

½ tsp. of Pepper

½ tsp. of Garlic Powder

¼ tsp. of Onion Powder

¼ tsp. of Cayenne Pepper

Directions:

1. In a small mixing bowl, mix all of the ingredients together well.
2. Store it in an airtight container.

Quick and Easy Taco Seasoning

Ingredients:

1 Tbsp. of Chili Powder

¼ tsp. of Garlic Powder

¼ tsp. of Onion Powder

¼ tsp. of Crushed Red Pepper Flakes

¼ tsp. of Dried Oregano

½ tsp. of Paprika

1 ½ tsp. of Ground Cumin

1 tsp. of Sea Salt

1 tsp. of Pepper

Directions:

1. In a small mixing bowl, mix all of the ingredients together well.
2. Store it in an airtight container.

Homemade Garam Masala Seasoning

Ingredients:

1 Tbsp. of Cumin

1 ½ tsp. Coriander

1 ½ tsp. of Cardamom

1 ½ tsp. of Pepper

1 tsp. of Cinnamon

½ tsp. of Cloves – Ground

½ tsp. of Nutmeg

Directions:

1. In a small mixing bowl, mix all of the ingredients together well.
2. Store it in an airtight container.

Criollo Seasoning

Ingredients:

2 Tbsp. of Onion Powder

1 Tbsp. of Garlic Powder

2 Tbsp. of Oregano

2 Tbsp. of Basil

1 Tbsp. of Thyme

1 Tbsp. of Pepper

1 Tbsp. of White Pepper

1 Tbsp. of Cayenne Pepper

5 Tbsp. of Paprika

3 Tbsp. of Salt

Directions:

1. In a small mixing bowl, mix all of the ingredients together well.
2. Store it in an airtight container.

Delicious Taco Seasoning

Ingredients:

1 ½ Tbsp. of Corn Flour

4 ½ tsp. of Chili Powder

½ tsp. of Onion Powder

½ tsp. of Garlic Powder

½ tsp. of Seasoned Salt

½ tsp. of Paprika

¼ tsp. of Cumin

½ tsp. of Garlic Salt

¼ tsp. of Sugar

1 tsp. of Dried Minced Onion

½ tsp. of Beef Bouillon Granules

¼ tsp. of Ground Red Pepper

600 g of Ground Beef – When Using

250 ml of Water – When Using

Directions:

1. In a small mixing bowl, mix all of the ingredients together well.
2. Store it in an airtight container.

Cajun Spice

Ingredients:

2 tsp. of Salt

2 tsp. of Garlic Powder

2 ½ tsp. of Paprika

1 tsp. of Pepper

1 tsp. of Onion Powder

1 tsp. of Cayenne Pepper

1 ¼ tsp. of Dried Oregano

1 ¼ tsp. of Dried Thyme

½ tsp. of Red Pepper Flakes

Directions:

1. In a small mixing bowl, mix all of the ingredients together well.
2. Store it in an airtight container.

Quick Cajun Seasoning

Ingredients:

2 ½ Tbsp. of Salt

1 Tbsp. of Oregano

1 Tbsp. of Paprika

1 Tbsp. of Cayenne Pepper

1 Tbsp. of Pepper

Directions:

1. In a small mixing bowl, mix all of the ingredients together well.
2. Store it in an airtight container.

Chicken Seasoning Spicy Style

Ingredients:

1 ½ tsp. of Sea Salt

1 tsp. of Basil

1 tsp. of Rosemary

½ tsp. of Garlic Powder

½ tsp. of Dry mustard Powder

½ tsp. of Paprika

½ tsp. of Pepper

½ tsp. of Dried Thyme

¼ tsp. of Celery seed

¼ tsp. of Dried Parsley

1/8 tsp. of Cumin

1/8 tsp. of Cayenne Pepper

1/8 tsp. of Chicken Bouillon Granules

Directions:

1. In a small mixing bowl, mix all of the ingredients together well.
2. Store it in an airtight container.

Sage Infused Italian Seasoning

Ingredients:

2 Tbsp. of Dried Basil

2 Tbsp. of Oregano

2 Tbsp. of Thyme

2 Tbsp. of Marjoram

1 Tbsp. of Rosemary

1 Tbsp. of Sage

Directions:

1. Use a food processor to thoroughly blend the ingredients.
2. Blend it for 1 minute.

Meat Seasoning

Ingredients:

2 Tbsp. of dried Minced Onion

2 ½ tsp. of Thyme

2 tsp. of Allspice

2 tsp. of Pepper

½ tsp. of Cinnamon

½ tsp. of Cayenne Pepper

½ tsp. of Salt

2 Tbsp. of Vegetable Oil – When Using

Directions:

1. In a small mixing bowl, mix all of the ingredients together well.
2. Store it in an airtight container.
3. When using, coat the meat with the oil and then rub the seasonings onto the meat.

Cumin Taco Seasoning

Ingredients:

30 g of Flour – Unbleached

75 g of Onion Flakes

1 tsp. of Minced Garlic

130 g of Chili Powder

2 tsp. of Oregano

2 tsp. of Cumin

4 tsp. of Salt

Directions:

1. In a small mixing bowl, mix all of the ingredients together well.
2. Store it in an airtight container.

Buttermilk Dressing

Ingredients:

30 g of Dry Buttermilk Powder

2 Tbsp. of Minced Onion – Dried

2 Tbsp. of Dried Parsley

1 Tbsp. of Dried Chives

¼ tsp. of Salt

1 tsp. of Garlic Powder

1 tsp. of Dried Celery Flakes

½ tsp. of White Pepper

¼ tsp. of Paprika

¼ tsp. of Dried Dill Weed

Directions:

1. In a small mixing bowl, mix all of the ingredients together well.
2. Store it in an airtight container.
3. Dressing: 500 g of Mayonnaise, 500 ml of Milk, and seasoning. Whisk it together well.

Chili-Free Taco Seasoning

Ingredients:

1 Tbsp. of Cumin

1 tsp. of Red Pepper Flakes

1 ½ tsp. of Paprika

1 tsp. of Oregano

2 tsp. of Garlic powder

½ tsp. of Onion Powder

1 ½ tsp. of Salt

1 ½ tsp. of Pepper

Directions:

1. In a small mixing bowl, mix all of the ingredients together well.
2. Store it in an airtight container.

Easy Apple Pie Seasoning

Ingredients:

4 tsp. of Cinnamon

2 tsp. of Nutmeg

1 tsp. of Cardamom

Directions:

1. In a small mixing bowl, mix all of the ingredients together well.
2. Store it in an airtight container.

Mild Curry Seasoning

Ingredients:

2 Tbsp. of Cumin

2 Tbsp. of Coriander

2 tsp. of Turmeric

½ tsp. of Crushed Red Pepper Flakes

½ tsp. of Mustard Seed

½ tsp. of Ground Ginger

Directions:

1. In a small mixing bowl, mix all of the ingredients together well.
2. Store it in an airtight container.

Mediterranean Spice Mix

Ingredients:

1 Tbsp. of Garlic Salt

1 Tbsp. of Onion Powder

1 Tbsp. of White Sugar

2 Tbsp. of Oregano

1 tsp. of Pepper

¼ tsp. of Thyme

1 tsp. of Basil

1 Tbsp. of Parsley

¼ tsp. of Celery Salt

2 Tbsp. of Salt

Directions:

1. In a small mixing bowl, add in all of the ingredients. Whisk them well.
2. To prepare the dressing, whisk 60 ml of white vinegar, 2 tbsp. of water, 200 ml of canola oil, and 2 Tbsp. of the mix.

Spanish Seasoning

Ingredients:

2 Tbsp. of Salt

1 Tbsp. of Paprika

2 tsp. of Pepper

1 ½ tsp. of Onion Powder

1 ½ tsp. of Oregano

1 ½ tsp. of Cumin

1 tsp. of Garlic Powder

1 tsp. of Chili Powder

Directions:

1. In a mixing bowl, stir in all of the ingredients very well using a whisk.
2. Store it in a sealed container in a cool, dry area.

BBQ Chili Rub

Ingredients:

140 g of Chili Powder

1 Tbsp. of Minced Garlic

1 tsp. of Onion Powder

½ tsp. of Cumin

1 ½ tsp. of Salt

2 Tbsp. of Seasoning Salt

900 g of Tomatoes Sauce

60 g of Brown Sugar

100 g of Fresh Tomato

¼ Tbsp. of Worcestershire Sauce

2 Tbsp. of Onion Flakes

70 g of Soy Sauce

60 ml of Water

Directions:

1. In a small mixing bowl, mix all of the ingredients together well.
2. Store it in an airtight container.
3. Don't add in the liquid ingredients until you are ready to use the sauce blend.

Hungarian Paprika-Chili-Mix

Ingredients:

40 g of Chili Powder

1 ½ Tbsp. of Cumin

4 tsp. of Onion Powder

4 tsp. of Paprika – Hungarian

2 tsp. of Garlic Powder

2 tsp. of Salt

2 tsp. of Onion Powder

1 tsp. of Dried Oregano

1 ½ tsp. of Brown Sugar

1 tsp. of Cayenne Pepper

1 tsp. of Mustard Powder

½ tsp. of Coriander

¼ tsp. of Pepper

Dash of Cinnamon

2 Bay Leaves

Directions:

1. In a small mixing bowl, mix all of the ingredients together well.
2. Store it in an airtight container.

Tasty Pizza Topping

Ingredients:

100 g of Parmesan Cheese – Grated

1 tsp. of Italian Seasoning

1 tsp. of Poultry Seasoning

1 tsp. of Cumin

¼ tsp. of Garlic Powder

Directions:

1. In a small mixing bowl, mix all of the ingredients together well.
2. Store it in an airtight container.
3. Keep it in the refrigerator and keep it for 2 months.

Hellenic Seasoning

Ingredients:

2 tsp. of Salt

2 tsp. of Garlic Powder

2 tsp. of Basil

2 tsp. of Greek Oregano

1 tsp. of Cinnamon

1 tsp. of Pepper

1 tsp. of Parsley

1 tsp. of Rosemary

1 tsp. of Dill Weed

1 tsp. of Marjoram

1 tsp. of Cornstarch

½ tsp. of Thyme

½ tsp. of Nutmeg

Directions:

1. In a small mixing bowl, mix all of the ingredients together well.
2. Store it in an airtight container.
3. Optional: Use a food processor to blend it very well.

Chicken Seasoning

Ingredients:

50 g of Parsley

25 g of Sage - Rubbed

15 g of Rosemary

15 g of Marjoram

2 Tbsp. of Salt

1 Tbsp. of Pepper

2 tsp. of Onion Powder

½ tsp. of Sage – Ground

Directions:

1. In a small mixing bowl, mix all of the ingredients together well.
2. Store it in an airtight container.

Rural Style Dressing

Ingredients:

1 tsp. of Dried Parsley

¾ tsp. of Pepper

1 tsp. of Seasoned Salt

½ tsp. of Garlic Powder

¼ tsp. of Onion Powder

1/8 tsp. of Dried Thyme

Directions:

1. In a small mixing bowl, mix all of the ingredients together well.
2. Store it in an airtight container.
3. Dressing: Mix 100 g of mayonnaise with 250 ml of buttermilk into the seasoning.
4. Dip: Mix the seasoning with 150 g of sour cream and 60 ml of buttermilk.

Paprika-Thyme-Seasoning

Ingredients:

1 ½ Tbsp. of Paprika

1 Tbsp. of Garlic Powder

1 Tbsp. of Onion Powder

1 Tbsp. of Dried Thyme

1 tsp. of Pepper

1 tsp. of Cayenne Pepper

1 tsp. of Dried Basil

1 sp. Of Dried Oregano

Directions:

1. In a small mixing bowl, mix all of the ingredients together well.
2. Store it in an airtight container.

Bread Crumbs Seasoning

Ingredients:

360 g of Bread Crumbs

100 ml of Vegetable Oil

1 Tbsp. of Salt

1 Tbsp. of Paprika

1 Tbsp. of Celery Salt

1 tsp. of Pepper

½ tsp. of Garlic Salt

½ tsp. of Minced Garlic

¼ tsp. of Minced Onion

1 Dash of Dried Basil Leaves

1 Dash of Dried Parsley

1 Dash of Dried Oregano

Directions:

1. In a large zip lock bag, combine the ingredients. Mix them very well.
2. Add in the meat to coat it with the seasonings.

Tex-Mex Seasoning

Ingredients:

1 Tbsp. of Cornstarch

2 tsp. of Chili Powder

1 tsp. of Salt

1 tsp. of Paprika

1 tsp. of White Sugar

½ tsp. of Onion Powder

½ tsp. of Garlic Powder

¼ tsp. of Cayenne Pepper

½ tsp. of Ground Cumin

Directions:

1. In a small mixing bowl, mix all of the ingredients together well.
2. Store it in an airtight container.

Onion-Garlic-Chilistyle-Mix

Ingredients:

1 Tbsp. of Paprika

2 ½ tsp. of Seasoning Salt

1 tsp. of Onion Powder

1 tsp. of Garlic Powder

1 tsp. of Cayenne Pepper

1 tsp. of Seasoned Pepper

½ tsp. of Thyme

½ tsp. of Dried Oregano

Directions:

1. In a small mixing bowl, mix all of the ingredients together well.
2. Store it in an airtight container.

Burger Seasoning

Ingredients:

1 Tbsp. of Paprika

1 ¼ tsp. of Salt

1 tsp. of Pepper

½ tsp. of Brown Sugar

½ tsp. of Garlic Powder

½ tsp. of Onion Powder

¼ tsp. of Cayenne Pepper

Directions:

1. In a small mixing bowl, mix all of the ingredients together well.
2. Store it in an airtight container.

Pumpkin Pie Flavour

Ingredients:

1 tsp. of Cinnamon

¼ tsp. of Nutmeg

¼ tsp. of Ginger

1/8 tsp. of Ground Cloves

Directions:

1. In a small mixing bowl, mix all of the ingredients together well.
2. Store it in an airtight container.

Acadia Spices

Ingredients:

200 g of Salt

¼ Cup of Cayenne Pepper

2 Tbsp. of White Pepper

2 Tbsp. of Pepper

2 Tbsp. of Paprika

2 Tbsp. of Onion Powder

2 Tbsp. of Garlic Powder

Directions:

1. In a small mixing bowl, mix all of the ingredients together well.
2. Store it in an airtight container.

Chicken Rub

Ingredients:

1 Tbsp. of Celery Flakes

1 Tbsp. of Salt

1 Tbsp. of Paprika

1 Tbsp. of Garlic Powder

1 Tbsp. of Onion Powder

1 Tbsp. of Thyme

2 tsp. of Dried Sage

1 ½ tsp. of Pepper

1 ½ tsp. of Dried Rosemary

½ tsp. of Cayenne Pepper

Directions:

1. In a small mixing bowl, mix all of the ingredients together well.
2. Store it in an airtight container.

Seafood Friendly Seasoning

Ingredients:

6 1/3 Tbsp. of Salt

3 2/3 Tbsp. of Celery Seed

2 ½ tsp. of Dry Mustard Powder

2 ½ tsp. of Red Pepper Flakes – Ground

1 ½ tsp. of Pepper

1 ½ tsp. of Bay Leaves – Ground

1 ½ tsp. of Paprika

1 tsp. of Ground Cloves

1 tsp. of Allspice

1 tsp. of Ground Ginger

¾ tsp. of Cardamom

½ tsp. of Cinnamon

Directions:

1. In a small mixing bowl, mix all of the ingredients together well.
2. Store it in an airtight container.

Herb Salt

Ingredients:

140 g of Sea Salt

A Handful of Rosemary Leaves

A Handful of Lemon Thyme Leaves

50 g of Table Salt

Directions:

1. In a small mixing bowl, mix all of the ingredients together well.
2. Allow it to air dry for 2-3 hours.
3. Store it in an airtight container.

Lamb Rub

Ingredients:

1 tsp. of Paprika

1 ½ tsp. of Thyme

1 ½ tsp. of Basil

¾ tsp. of Cumin

2 Tbsp. of Curry Powder

Directions:

1. In a small mixing bowl, mix all of the ingredients together well.
2. Store it in an airtight container.

Chili Seasoning Blend

Ingredients:

2 Tbsp. of Chili Powder

1 tsp. of Paprika

1 tsp. of Cayenne Pepper

½ tsp. of Salt

½ tsp. of Black and Red Pepper Mix

½ tsp. of Garlic Powder

1/3 tsp. of Cumin

¼ tsp. of Nutmeg

Directions:

1. In a small mixing bowl, mix all of the ingredients together well.
2. Store it in an airtight container.

Mare Mediterraneum Seasoning

Ingredients:

2 Tbsp. of Salt

2 Tbsp. of Coriander

2 Tbsp. of Cinnamon

1 Tbsp. of Cumin

1 Tbsp. of Nutmeg

1 Tbsp. of Pepper

Directions:

1. In a small mixing bowl, mix all of the ingredients together well.
2. Store it in an airtight container.
3. Rub it on the meat 30 minutes before you cook it.

Pickling Spices

Ingredients:

2 Tbsp. of Whole Mustard Seeds

1 Tbsp. of Allspice Berries

2 tsp. of Coriander Seeds

1 tsp. of Red Pepper Flakes

1 tsp. of Ginger – Ground

2 Bay Leaves

2 Cinnamon Sticks

6 Whole Cloves

Directions:

1. In a small mixing bowl, mix all of the ingredients together well.
2. Use a food processor to blend it very well.
3. Store it in an airtight container.

Ground Beef Taco Seasoning

Ingredients:

1 Tbsp. of Onion Flakes

1 tsp. of Flour

1 tsp. of Beef Bouillon Granules

1 tsp. of Garlic Salt

1 tsp. of Cumin

1 tsp. of Paprika

1 tsp. of Chili Powder

¼ tsp. of Cayenne Pepper

¼ tsp. of White Sugar

Directions:

1. In a small mixing bowl, mix all of the ingredients together well.
2. Store it in an airtight container.
3. Enough seasoning for 500 g of ground beef.

Oatmeal Flavour

Ingredients:

250 ml of Nonfat Dry Milk Powder

200 g of Sugar

150 g of Brown Sugar

2 tsp. of Salt

1 tsp. of Cinnamon

½ tsp. of Pumpkin Pie Spice

½ tsp. of Nutmeg

½ tsp. of Cardamom

Directions:

1. In a small mixing bowl, mix all of the ingredients together well.
2. Store it in an airtight container.
3. Use: Add in enough water to the consistency of your choosing. Boil the water first so that your oatmeal is hot and ready.

Fish Seasoning

Ingredients:

1 Tbsp. of Basil

1 Tbsp. of Crushed Rosemary

1 Tbsp. of Parsley

2 tsp. of Sea Salt

2 tsp. of Pepper

2 tsp. of Dried Sage

2 tsp. of Thyme

2 tsp. of Marjoram

1 tsp. of Oregano

1 tsp. of Celery Salt

1 tsp. of Garlic Powder

Directions:

1. In a small mixing bowl, mix all of the ingredients together well.
2. Store it in an airtight container.
3. Use: Rub it on your fish before you cook it.

Carribean Curry Blend

Ingredients:

20 g of Whole Coriander Seeds

2 Tbsp. of Whole Cumin Seeds

2 Tbsp. of Whole Anise Seeds

1 Tbsp. of Whole Fenugreek Seeds

1 Tbsp. of Whole Allspice Berries

5 Tbsp. of Turmeric

Directions:

1. In a small mixing bowl, mix all of the ingredients together well.
2. Use a food processor to blend it very well.
3. Store it in an airtight container.

Ginger-Garlic-Paste

Ingredients:

120 g of Garlic – Chopped

120 g of Ginger – Chopped

1 Tbsp. of Olive Oil

Directions:

1. Add in all of the ingredients in a food processor.
2. Use it immediately.

Popcorn Seasoning

Ingredients:

¼ tsp. Of Onion Powder

¼ tsp. of Dill Weed

1/8 tsp. of Garlic Powder

1/8 tsp. of Salt

1/8 tsp. of Pepper

1/8 tsp. of Vegetable Oil

Directions:

1. Mix it all very well and pour it on the popcorn.
2. Toss the popcorn to ensure that it is coated well.

Pinyin Five-Spices

Ingredients:

30 g of Whole Star Anise Pods

5 Tbsp. of Whole Cloves

5 Tbsp. of Szechuan Peppercorns

5 Tbsp. of Fennel Seed

40 g of Cinnamon

Directions:

1. In a small mixing bowl, mix all of the ingredients together well.
2. Use a food processor to blend it very well.
3. Store it in an airtight container.

Image sources/Printing information

Pictures cover: depositphotos.com;

@IgorTishenko; @ VickyDimBO; @ AntonMatyukha; @ BrunoWeltmann

Print edition black and white paperback:

Amazon Media EU S.à.r.l.

5 Rue Plaetis

L-2338 Luxembourg

Other printouts:

epubli, a service of neopubli GmbH, Berlin

Publisher:

BookRix GmbH & Co. KG

Sonnenstraße 23

80331 München

Deutschland

Printed in Great Britain
by Amazon